Also by Tim Dlugos

High There (Some of Us Press, 1973)
For Years (Jawbone, 1977)
Je Suis Ein Americano (Little Caesar Press, 1979)
A Fast Life (Sherwood Press, 1982)
Entre Nous (Little Caesar Press, 1982)
G-9 (Hanuman Books, 1992)

STRONG PLACE

STRONG PLACE

poems by
TIM DLUGOS

Introduction by David Trinidad

Amethyst Press
New York

Copyright © 1992 by the estate of Tim Dlugos
Introduction copyright © 1992 by David Trinidad
A list of acknowledgments appears on page 87

The estate of Tim Dlugos wishes to thank Duncan Hannah,
Ken Schwartz, Ira Silverberg, and David Trinidad.

All rights reserved. No part of this book may be reproduced in
any form without permission in writing from the publisher,
except by a reviewer, who may quote brief passages in a review.

Printed in the United States of America

LIBRARY OF CONGRESS CATALOGING-IN-PUBLICATION DATA

Dlugos, Tim.
  Strong Place : poems / by Tim Dlugos : introduction by
David Trinidad.
      p.   cm.
  ISBN 0-927200-13-9 (soft cover) : $9.95
  1. Gay men—Poetry. 2. AIDS (Disease)—Poetry. I. Title.
PS3554.L48S77   1992
811'.54—dc20   92-9223
                                                    CIP

Laser typography by Michael Mele, Brooklyn, New York

Amethyst Press
70-A Greenwich Avenue, No. 102
New York, New York 10011

FIRST PRINTING

for Christopher Wiss

CONTENTS

Introduction by David Trinidad *xiii*

I.

Close *3*
Sonnet *5*
Film *6*
On This Train Are People Who Resemble *7*
Spinner *8*
Song *9*
Not Stravinsky *10*
Summer, South Brooklyn *11*
From Journal *12*
Solidarity *14*
Harding's Beach *17*
New Music *19*
From Journal *20*
Psalm *21*

II.

The Morning *25*
A Sense *27*
The Nineteenth Century Is 183 Years Old *28*
Octavian *29*
Four Organs *32*
Pretty Convincing *33*
This Much Fun *36*

III. King of the Wood

"Know you not / your father's house and name?" *41*
"In which meaning is a quantity," *43*
"Night goes up in . . . smoke? No, fog." *45*
"Go gently into that good morning," *46*
"O say, can you see?" *47*
"Fresh as red air of Tuscany, the dawn" *48*
To Walter Lowenfels *51*
"Hercules becomes Celestial" *53*
"Exult now, all you angels and archangels," *55*
Where Is Art? *57*
"Old man, look at my life" *59*
October *60*
"Dear Heart, wish you or I were here or there . . ." *61*

IV.

Cape and Islands *65*
The Fruit Streets *73*
Desire Under the Pines *75*
Lit *76*
Words For Simone Weil *77*
July *78*
Healing the World From Battery Park *81*

INTRODUCTION

Tim Dlugos and I first met in 1981, the year he began to
write the poems in this book. Tim had come to Los Angeles,
where I was living then, to read in Dennis Cooper's series at
Beyond Baroque Literary/Arts Center. I attended this read-
ing and was blown away, as many of us were, by his work.
Except for Dennis, who was rapidly making a name for
himself, everyone in the Beyond Baroque "gang" (Amy
Gerstler, Bob Flanagan, Jack Skelley, and others) was just
starting out. In our eyes, Tim was the epitome of the
sophisticated urban poet: he lived in Manhattan, where *it*
was happening; he brushed elbows with many of our heroes
(including the ghost of Frank O'Hara); his writing, although
influenced by the New York School, displayed a candor,
ingenuity, and wit that was distinctly his own. He was also
one of the best openly gay poets around, miles ahead of that
throng of boy-loving bards who'd thrived during the libera-
tion boom of the seventies. I was particularly moved by two
of the poems Tim read that night: "Gilligan's Island" (which
brilliantly employs images from the sixties TV show, the
movie *The Birds*, and the assassination of J.F.K.) and
"Pastorale," an elegy for his friend Virgil Moore: "Update:
Mary Ellen is a therapist in Center / City. John is a
professional actor (so what else / is new, you'd say), Jack is
married, Kevin / is divorced. I'm a writer living in New
York." At the time, I was struggling to recover from the
death of my friend, the poet Rachel Sherwood (I was, in fact,
in the process of establishing a small press in her name), so
"Pastorale" affected me deeply. The casual yet poignant
tone of Tim's poem gave me hope that I might one day
reconcile my own loss.

At the reception afterwards (prompted by Dennis, as I
was terribly shy), I introduced myself to Tim and excitedly

thanked him for his reading. Tim was very gracious, and very talkative—a good thing, since after my initial gush I couldn't think of another word to say. I simply stood there, sipping white wine from my plastic cup, nervously nodding and glancing from Tim's glasses (and the animated greenish-blue eyes behind them) to his receding hairline, to the collar of his pin-striped shirt, tucked neatly into his collegiate sweater. I must have said *something* because we made plans to get together before he returned to New York. I floated out of Beyond Baroque like a fan who'd just won a date with his favorite movie star.

Tim was staying at the Tropicana on Santa Monica Boulevard in West Hollywood, within walking distance of a number of trendy gay bars. He loved the sleazy glamour of the motel and proudly identified the rooms in which certain rock stars had once slept. His own room was littered with clothes, papers, and books. The telephone sat prominently on the rumpled bedspread, next to his rolodex, which he'd brought from New York. He'd also brought his portable manual typewriter; I tried to sneak a peek at the half-finished poem sticking out of it. We ate lunch at a restaurant above the Sunset Strip, then spent the afternoon talking and driving around in his rental car. On one street, Tim slowed down and pointed out the carport where Sal Mineo had been stabbed to death—how like Tim to give me a tour of my own city. As it got dark, we decided to spend the evening "on the town." After hanging around his motel room (waiting, of course, for an appropriate hour to show our faces), we proceeded to hit every bar in the neighborhood. There were lots of beautiful boys to look at and lots of cocktails to order; we continued to do both until "last call." Walking Tim back to the Tropicana, I told him how much I admired him and his poetry, and how moved I'd been by his reading of "Pastorale." A few days after Tim flew home, I received an inscribed copy of the poem, along with a note—on

Tropicana stationery. "I had the most *wonderful* time with you yesterday," he wrote. "It was a day of discovery on a lot of levels—and the beginning, I hope, of a good friendship."

Our friendship developed long-distance, in letters and phone conversations full of shoptalk, gossip, and personal news. One night early on, Tim called me and announced that he was spending the evening in bed, with a bottle of bourbon. When I told him I was doing the same, only with scotch, he erupted with laughter. Tim loved to laugh, especially at his own witticisms, of which he had a limitless supply. His laugh was convulsive, contagious too—you couldn't help but join in, even if you hadn't gotten the joke. He always had a new poem on hand and would ask in that mock-coy voice of his (because he knew you weren't going to say no): "I wrote a new poem today. Wanna hear it?" That's one thing I will always miss: Tim reading his latest poem to me on the telephone.

In the spring of 1982, Tim's first full-length book of poems, *Entre Nous*, was published by Dennis' Little Caesar Press. At the same time, I put out his long poem "A Fast Life" as a Sherwood Press chapbook. Tim came back to L.A. (and to a room at the Tropicana) for a grand publication party and reading. The party was at Dennis' apartment on Overland Avenue. I was pretty drunk that night; most of it's a blur. I do remember that John Doe, an old friend of Tim's from Washington, D.C. and a member of the rock group X, showed up with his lead singer Exene, so Tim was in his element—among the famous. (Tim and John Doe, by the way, share a joint on page 74.) Amy Gerstler wore a red dress; I remember making out with her in the kitchen. Later, Dennis poured a drink on my head, which infuriated me. I left in a huff and drove home in a blackout. Around noon the next day, Tim called to report that after the party he'd had "an incredible adventure." Driving across town, he'd picked up a hustler on Santa Monica Boulevard and brought him back to the Tropicana, where Tim promptly passed out. When he came to, he discovered that the hustler had split with all of his money *and* his favorite sweater. Despite the theft (and a terrific hangover), Tim was obviously delighted: he had a new story to tell. And as hung over as I was, I loved hearing it. This was, after all, what poets were supposed to do, right? Weren't such "adventures" the stuff of future literary biographies?

Later that year, when I visited New York for the first time, Tim put me up in his apartment at 31 Strong Place in Brooklyn. The address had special significance for him: 31 (his age when he'd moved there the previous year) Strong Place (a level of accomplishment he felt he'd reached in his poetry). Tim's apartment was full of art (Trevor Winkfield, Joe Brainard, Duncan Hannah, a collage by poet Alice Notley) and shelves that supported substantial book and record collections. His taste in music was eclectic: Puccini's *Turandot* and Joni Mitchell's *Court and Spark* could easily slap together on his turntable. It was a whirlwind trip of readings, parties, openings, and running to bars. Tim gave me many tours of Manhattan, pointing to this or that landmark; it was impossible to take it all in. He was so excited by New York and its history, still thrilled after six years to be, as the song goes, a part of it. One morning, however, I encountered an angry host. When I woke up on the fold-out couch, Tim loomed over me, hands on his hips like a stern mom. "You drink too much," he reprimanded. The night before, I'd finished off all the alcohol in the house; he'd just discovered the empty beer and scotch bottles I'd tried to hide in the trash. It was a painful yet important moment. As much as Tim's words hurt, they prompted me to begin addressing the problem I'd succeeded in avoiding for many years.

Tim's next (and last) trip to Los Angeles was in May of '84. By then, Dennis was living in Manhattan, and the two of them flew out together to give a reading at Beyond Baroque. I was a mere six months sober and still pretty shaky; every night, I attended an 11:30 support group for recovering alcoholics. It was to this meeting that I drove after hearing Tim read "Pretty Convincing," a poem in which he admits to having a drinking problem. For the first time, in fact, I noticed that his drinking was out of control. There were several "scenes" that trip, all centered around a boy that he and Dennis were vying for. It was a bit like a situation comedy: Tim would call to complain about Dennis; then, a few minutes later, Dennis would call to complain about Tim—throwing in a barb about Tim's drinking. On Mother's Day, the day before he was to leave, Tim called and informed me that that morning he'd been to his first A.A. meeting. He'd actually liked it (It had helped, he confessed, that there'd been some cute boys in the room) and wanted to give sobriety a chance. That night, I took him to my late meeting. It must have been a full moon: everyone was carrying on like extras in *Marat/Sade*—mumbling to themselves, gesturing wildly, shouting. Someone even threw a chair across the room. I wanted Tim to get a good impression of recovery and kept apologizing for everyone's crazy behavior. "It's not usually like this," I insisted. But Tim wasn't deterred at all. He loved every minute of it.

Tim returned to New York and stayed sober. Occasionally, he'd call with a progress report. He completed the *Strong Place* manuscript and started sending it around to some publishers. It was, as so much good poetry is, rejected by all of them. Somewhat discouraged, Tim put his poetry on the back burner for a while. In July of '86, he met his last lover, Christopher Wiss, on Fire Island. (Tim and Chris remained together until Tim's death; it was, as Tim has written, his "first / healthy and enduring relationship / in sobriety.") That fall, Tim moved from Strong Place to the rectory at the Church of Saint Mary the Virgin on West 47th

Street, fondly referred to as "Smoky Mary's," where he lived for the next two years. The spiritual aspect of recovery intensified his desire to become an Episcopal priest. In order to qualify for the graduate program at Yale Divinity School (a big dream of Tim's was to attend that prestigious university), he enrolled at Hunter College to finish his B.A. Although puzzled by Tim's need to pursue a traditionally religious life (one which seemed antithetical to a gay, or even an "artistic," lifestyle), I was reminded that religion had always been important to him. It's in many of his poems. "Psalm," for instance, beautifully captures the sincerity of his spiritual quest.

The following September was difficult for Tim. First, his mother died on Labor Day. Tim, who'd been adopted, was close to his parents (his father had died a few years before, while Tim was still drinking) and their deaths hit him pretty hard. Then, that same month, Tim found out that he was HIV positive. I remember him calling with the bad news. His T-cell count was alarmingly low, but when I expressed concern he got defensive. His denial was only beginning to break; it would take him a while to talk about the state of his health with a certain amount of acceptance. There was good news too: I was planning to move to New York, and we were both happy that, at last, we would live in the same city. Ironically, by the time I did move, in the summer of '88, he had been accepted by Yale Divinity School and had just relocated to Connecticut. My first week in New York, Tim picked me up and drove me, in the car he'd inherited from his mother, to New Haven. He showed me his apartment on Rowe Street and, forever the tour guide, familiarized me with the campus. After I bought a Yale T-shirt (a detail Tim later put in one of his poems), we ate hamburgers at a student hangout. Tim was taking AZT and on the drive back, when I questioned him about his health, he spoke angrily about AIDS and its effect on all of our lives. What struck me, on this rare occasion when Tim let his guard down, was his honesty about the devastating effect of his own HIV status.

The last two years of his life, Tim and I kept in close contact. He was often in Manhattan, and we'd eat, look at art, or go to A.A. meetings together. He was writing regularly again; frequently, he'd call and read me a new poem, then send a copy so I could see it on the page. After he was diagnosed with AIDS in mid '89, Tim produced his best work—stunning poems dealing with his illness and his impending death, many of which were written while he was recuperating from pneumocystis pneumonia on G-9, the AIDS ward at Roosevelt Hospital. It was painful to watch Tim's health deteriorate. He lost weight, covered the KS lesions on his face with little round Band-Aids, and periodically used a cane. Yet he rarely complained; he was making the most of what time he had left. He continued with his studies at Yale, wrote incredible poems, flew to San Francisco to present a talk at a gay and lesbian writers conference, traveled to Europe with Chris, and kept in touch with his many friends. He was even editing his own literary magazine—called, appropriately enough, *Tim*. Sadly, that project was never completed. In the summer of 1990, he worked as a hospital chaplain at Jersey City Medical Center and found the experience immensely gratifying. He loved spending time with the patients and beamed when he talked about it. He'd realized yet another of his dreams.

On October 31st, Tim appeared on *Good Morning America* (in a segment about artists with AIDS) and read from his poems: "I feel so confident / most days that I can stay / alive, survive and thrive / with AIDS." A couple of weeks later, he was admitted to Roosevelt Hospital for the last time. I visited him on November 27th, in the late afternoon. He was using an oxygen mask and it was hard for him to talk, but we managed to have a conversation. He dozed off several times, and I sat holding his hand, trying to think of what to say when he opened his eyes again. I wanted to say something profound, but my mind kept going blank. Finally, after a long silence, I said, "I love you, Tim." He squeezed my hand and, polite as ever, said, "It's nice of you to say so." At another point, he instructed, "Don't lose any of the poems I sent you." I assured him I wouldn't. The room had slowly grown dark and, before I left, he asked me to turn on a light behind his bed. I told him I'd visit again; he didn't respond, as if he knew that I wouldn't be able to. He died at 9:00 p.m. the following Monday, December 3, 1990. With him were his brother John, his friends Edgar Wells and Arthur Wolsoncroft, and Chris. He was forty years old.

Strong Place has not been abridged, nor have poems been added to it. It is the exact version that Tim wrote and compiled. Indeed, it contains some of his strongest work: "Spinner," "Psalm," "Harding's Beach," the outrageous "Pretty Convincing," "July," "Healing the World From Battery Park," and the long elegy for his father, "King of the Wood." I love his brazen wordplay, his impeccable rhymes, his cascading sentences, and his Pop interjections—those moments when high and low art seem to meet with a delightful, cartoonish crash:

> I'll lead you
> to a land of colors—Cranberry, Pineapple,
> Orange and the spurious Joralemon—and thrilling
> tastes. The rawness of the wind is softened
> by a blast of citrus, as the view
> from the Heights gains pigment with a flick
> of the Tint dial. It's a new world
> out there, as if a box of Trix
> had spilled across the harbor where the grays
> and silvers played beneath a sky they perfectly
> resembled.
>
>   ("The Fruit Streets")

See how the white turns pale blue as the night
creeps in, full of mosquitoes and fireflies.
And don't be frightened by the strangled cries
from the swamp; those are peepers bellowing,
not *Psycho III*.

("July")

Unlike many contemporary poets who fashionably strive to obscure narrative or to *not* make sense, Tim never abandoned his story. "I risk playing the fool," he says in "The Morning," "because this is a world I am creating, / not 'text' or 'slice of life,' and old contexts / don't hold." In more than five hundred poems (an amazing output spanning twenty dedicated years), Tim created his world, and it's a privilege for me, as a reader and friend, to be part of it. *Strong Place* is just a portion of the larger picture; the poems in this volume represent, if you will, a kind of middle period. Shortly before his death, Tim collected his last poems in a manuscript entitled *Powerless*. To date, this book—a remarkable record of individual courage and faith— has not found a publisher. I believe that it will. I also believe that Tim's work will receive the recognition it so clearly deserves.

David Trinidad
New York City
January 1992

STRONG PLACE

I.

Close

FOR BRAD GOOCH

Spring peaks: the third of May, the feast of Love.
Cherry flowers old, magnolias new.
Peahens chase tots in the cathedral close.
We share a therapist, up there three stories.
I'm here to recollect, and recollect I shall,
but first let me get over this amazing blue

of sky above new green of leaves and blue
of polyester running shoes. I love
to think it's something absolutely new,
this light and weather, like my summer clothes,
but they predate us both, say histories.
Pretending it's the first time is a shell

game. Can't beat Demon Time, they say, though Shel-
ley disagreed. The rains came, the winds blew
and swamped his tiny boat. I'm not in love
with impiety, just with youth. The new
world is a-comin', old draws to a close,
a row of vignettes pasted on a story-

board by young go-getters with success stories
and salable today, beneath the shel-
tering deciduous to kids in blue-
jeans, teenaged like the leaves, amazed by love
that sprouts like sudden flowers on their new
embarrassed shapes. Their childhood's at a close,

a time they thought the doors would never close
behind them or before them, as in stories
on *Time Tunnel* or *Twilight Zone*. They shall
learn differently. It used to make me blue
to think of it, but now it makes me love
great days like this one with a giddy new

intensity. It *is* completely new,
this light, that five-year-old with his fat close-
mouthed nurse, that row of petals three long stories
above my head, where you are. And they shall
never be quite the same again; the blue
sky either, or you, or I. That's why love

"makes all things new." Beats history. This bloo-
ming close opens my shell to Love, to you.

Sonnet

Stevie Nicks walks into the Parisian weather
in Brooklyn where the "heat wave"'s mild
December 3rd and waiting for the Child
who's born and laid upon the oxen's plate

of straw again, bound up again in swaddling
clothes in Health-Tex patterns, and projecting
good vibes the way Matt Dillon looks onscreen
shirt off and washboard stomach   when I'm waddling

home I think of him   the Teenage Fates
in chorus chant, "You wish"   I do, rejecting
sagacity in favor of new leather
and what's inside, a-tremble at the clean

wet silver sky and street   the natives tout it,
cool light, slim trees   there's something French about it

Film

Buildup of the sudden snow on nested ships
Obscured by the wet snow blowing horizontal
Faster when it's closer, slower at the plane
Where it fades into undistinguished film
Illustrating theories of physics or the best
Of background animation, early Disney as opposed
To cheapo imitations from Japan   My Task:
To flesh out the cartoon of the morning,
My white walls, blank stare   Eno's
Film Music extricated from white jacket
Think of Melville as it fills the air

On This Train Are People Who Resemble

Allen Ginsberg
President Carter
Lynne Dreyer
Geraldine Fitzgerald
a monkey
Brian Epstein
Don Bachardy
the son on "Sanford and Son"
Rose Lesniak
Mrs. Sanders (neighbor, 1966)
Erin Clermont
Sid Caesar in drag
Terry Bartek (wrestling partner, high school gym class)
"Dad" on "Dennis the Menace" — in fact, I think it *is* Dad, "Henry
                        Mitchell," grayer and with deep
                        lines in his face but the same
                        receding chin and purse-mouthed but
                        benevolent expression, in a summer
                        suit that's old but neatly pressed
                        and clunky black shoes. He wears
                        a sad expression, too, and I wonder
                        if life has been unkind to him,
                        thinking how awful it would be to
                        have a third-rate sitcom as the
                        crowning achievement of your artistic
                        career, to be reduced to taking the
                        subway and having people recognize
                        you (if you're lucky) for the wimp
                        you played, maybe remembering the name
                        of the smirking brat who played your son
                        (Jay North) but never yours or any of
                        the program's other grownups, who by now
                        are dead (Mr. Wilson, R.I.P.) or grayheads
                        like you. I'd look sad too, I think, as
                        he walks out of the car at Penn Station.

Spinner

If Plato's right, my "you" is a reflection
of years-ago phenomena, the way I felt
when faced with your unquenchable erection
and well of nervous energy, that let you belt

the latest songs and dance till sunrise,
high as a kite whose string I held. You were as sweet
as your nightly two desserts, as unwise
as I, and just as loath to meet

unpleasantness head-on, as when you told me
that we were through. "Impossible," I said,
a disbelief that still enfolds me
when I wake and remember that you're dead.

I'm writing to your shadow, which recedes
with youth we shared and spent, to fill
the absence of your voice, my dull need.
Ghost of a ghost, this puts you farther still.

Song

Early summer sunlight and the wise guys whistle
(Squad car down the block) to let the dealers know
Under brims of cocoanut and baku
By the subway steps old men play dominoes

Salsa in the shade, the junk trees verdant
Empty lots that suddenly are full
Of city flora, as if broken glass were mulch
Pollen and the bus fumes make my own eyes swell

Underneath the footfalls, trains go uptown, downtown
Nothing out of place here, not a note or hair
Doesn't take a seer to spot a sucker
Cotton suit and boater in the shimmering air

Not Stravinsky

Dark-eyed boy in tight designer jeans and sneakers on your way
from basketball practice at Bishop Somebody High, I

don't know what you're playing on your Walkman but it probably is
not Stravinsky.

Summer, South Brooklyn

gusher in the street where bald men with cigars
watch as boys in gym shorts and no shirts
crack the hydrant, rinsing yet another car
a daily ritual, these street-wide spurts

of city water over rich brown and deep white
of ranch wagon and arrogant sedan
whose "opera windows" seem less *arriviste* than trite
they shake the water from their hair, shake hands

with neighbors passing, passing generations
I watch and am not part of, for the block is theirs
by family and tradition, and I'm no relation
an opera drowned by disco beat, draw stares

from big boys with big radios that might outlast them
brace myself for insults I recall
forgetting the adult they see when I stride past them
until I realize they're kids, that's all

From Journal

Picking up background material for a copy assignment at
Sanky's, I pass a desk and there's Terry, S.'s former assistant,
whom I haven't seen in years. Terry! It's been years! Tim!
she exclaims, and we reminisce about our first meeting, my
first New York employment interview, at Planned Parenthood
for Sanky's old job. It must be ten years ago, Terry says, and
when I correct her (five) she doesn't believe me, possibly
because she thinks I look ten years older says my intrusive
vanity. Terry doesn't look a day older. She's been out of the
industry; she and her husband retired to their dream house in
Front Royal, Virginia, two years ago. What's she doing back
in New York? Well, she falters, I lost my husband five
months ago . . . . I'm sorry, and tell her so; tell her also about
my father's death two weeks ago, my mother's loss similar to
hers: husband passing too short a time after they'd reached
their retirement destination, miles from friends and familiar
landscapes. Terry's back in town scouting possible jobs and
Staten Island apartments. She might move back and share a
place with her sister, but there's a snag: What'll I do with my
furniture? It's all valuable antiques. She alternately glares
and looks at me imploringly as she ticks off the pieces. A
marble-topped coffee table! A beautiful mahogany dining-
room set! Twin beds made extra-long especially (my husband
was six-feet-two, eyes tearing up)! A combination bench and
coat rack with the original mirror! The classic sideboard!
She's starting to get worked up. Then the trouble of moving
it all! The week they moved to Virginia, she broke her arm,
her husband almost had a second heart attack, and the cat
developed cancer. When they arrived in Front Royal, she had
to locate an orthopedist, a cardiologist and a vet. The husband
and the cat died. They sold their house in Cobble Hill,
occupied for five years by a couple of young men who called
Terry "Ma" (she pauses to see if I get the idea), so she can't

go back to Brooklyn. It's a dilemma, and she wants to know how my mother is facing what she perceives to be a similar crisis. By staying put for awhile, I say, and Terry agrees that the first months alone are the hardest, no time to make a big decision. She asks how my father died, and when I tell her (the sudden massive heart attack, the coma that looked as though it would last for months, and the quiet, equally unexpected death), she tells me, it's better than his being a vegetable. He had a vegetable *garden*, I want to say, but instead reply that I don't know how impaired he would have been, but he was a grumpy patient even when he had a cold (she nods; *men*, she thinks), so a long serious illness would have been awful for him, thereby setting up an opposition between death and discomfort, choosing the former, though neither I nor more importantly my father believed in that sort of glibness, and it's his life we're discussing, six stories over Times Square this gorgeous afternoon.

Solidarity

FOR JANE DE LYNN

As a white male Republican
who grew up in a middle middle class
environment and went to private schools,
I cherish my impediments: Polish, college
dropout, queer, which make me individual
but don't make me a victim

I have cousins I don't even know
facing down the tanks (or so
I like to think) in Poland where the air's
as white with snow as here
I care about them not as individuals
but as victims of the things we never faced
as individuals

           maybe that's why you can say
that you don't give a fuck about the Polacks
that when the Jews your people were marched off
into the winter, it was Polacks
my people who held the bayonets
for centuries, so why
should you give a fuck

I don't know what it's like to be a Jew,
but I know what it's like not to be one:
in my Viking hat and foreskin, washing down
my mastodon steak with milk while outnumbered
humanists, scholars of God's word, huddle
on their island of civility every time I belch

that is an illusion   another
is that my life or yours is normal
if these are normal times we should retire the word
for total action   we are on an outlaw island
privileged to speak sincerely

———

and be loud about it, our necks
aren't on the block

a privilege purchased with the sweat
of other individuals, our forebears   till the day
he died, my father called his childhood buddies Jewboys
they called him a Polack   they'd grown up
in the Bottom, wooden houses
crammed between the river and the railroad tracks
in Middletown   my father's sister's
sharpest memory of childhood's of her mother
looking out the attic window toward the river
where her sons and their friends
the Jewboys were stranded on a raft, halfway
to Portland, with stormclouds blowing down
the Connecticut, the dull reports
of thunder growing louder

there is no safety from the storm in huddling
with illusions that our privilege is anything
other than a raft
people facing tanks are victims
and the tanks are driven by average Joes
saving the world for normality

you're my kind of person   and it's your individual
traits that provoke my fondness, even when you
piss me off   but I feel responsible,
able to respond, when the cousins I don't even
know dodge the lightning   I have cousins
I don't even like, like you do
it's easier to take them when they're part
of a whole, a people, but that's not what I mean
by Solidarity — I mean that I can feel
responsible even when they're not my cousins
but yours, and that it's a right I assume,
unpurchased by another individual's
sweat   if we are to make

a history, we must be the source
not a cork that bobs on the ancestral stream
I choose solidarity with them and you
though I'm not a Jew, but a Polack

when the Ghetto Fighters rose up
in '43, Jew and Pole fought side by side
until they were mowed down by the tanks
that leveled the city they shared

when we share this city we are
friends, not victims   history's an impediment
only when I can't shed tears   when I see
red on the sidewalk I cannot recognize
whose blood it is from the color   the normal
weather buries it   where we are
it's snowing heavily

Harding's Beach

The families, the summer
visitors in sporty cars,
the bars, the short-lived
culture of the rays: peel them away
and it all boils down to colors.
To paint them is to lose them. Half
an hour from the dropping of the sun behind
the clouds, or haze, or smoke from a faraway
tragedy above the solid cottages that punctuate
the scrub due west, and almanac sunset.
In that interval, the wheel slows or perception
speeds up with the circling terns.
The train brakes at the dark green
suburbs of blue, and continues through
to the shadows on the other side. Grass
brushed back like a kewpie's forelock,
miles of it, and an impossible tangle
of kelp that describes the interval from moss
to brown, life to garbage. It's a simple
world for a gangly plant with big cells.
A boy fishes; then he goes away
to rest. A father and a son
stroll past the abandoned lighthouse
whose lamp room has been sheared off
with surgical skill. The boosters call it
"local color," but for now old stories
of seagods' bowler hats with razor brims
and architecture are an insubstantial gloss
on depths of fading light. Consolidates
then goes away, but leaves a scar.
The nests of terns are scratches in the sand,
no more. They flee at any sign of danger
and leave their eggs to boil, a vanishing race.

The cracking of a shell beneath a shoe, the beach
that used to be a billion shells, the shell
shaped like an ear trumpet locked inside
its strongbox for the night, and still
you hear the ocean.

New Music

The lovemaking grows more intense, not less.
Ten million men and women out of work
The price of a sound currency. Tim Page
Brings us "The New, The Old, The Unexpected,"
Two hours of new music every day,
Six hours of sleep, eight of work, and art
Simmers on the back burner with desire
For Fame, for Fortune. Rules: choose one, not both.

The reasons for not moving grow more lame.
Ten million stories in this naked city
And one of them is ours. I'm like Tim Miller
Spraying my name in paint upon my chest,
Reminding me of who I am. A man
By any other name's a refugee.
I shall not back away, but take my stand
Where love and honesty are one, not both.

It gets more complicated with the years
And less so. There must be ten million ways
Of making love, but all I need are three:
The new, the old, the unexpected. Grace
Is like New Music hitting with the force
Of tidal waves, or like the atmosphere
So clear these mornings we forget it's how
We've always lived and breathed as one, not both.

I touch you on the eyes, and chest, and wrist.
Ten million dollars wouldn't change a thing,
The price of a sound mind. "Tim Dlugos knows,"
Voice-over from an old-time radio
Reminding me of where I used to be.
I'm here, and so are you. To make it art
Is easy when you're musical as we.
Live it or live with it: choose one, not both.

From Journal

On most perfect sunny morning of the year, most perfect that could be imagined, walk down Strong Place to my landlady's cheeriest greeting. This is my neighborhood, and elitist gripes about living "so far away" seem dumb now. Look at those trees, those shadows (and their absence) — not that I have anything against the elite.

At St. Peter and Paul's Church ("the oldest free-standing steeple in Brooklyn") the doors are wide open. A funeral inside. No procession, just the line of limos that always makes me think of the Mafia or the Vice-President until I see the hearse. Codger on the corner shouts affectionately, "Well hello, Mary," and a potato-faced woman in her seventies says, "Hiya." Brooklyn is the home of thousands of Marys — used to have to be the middle name at least of every Catholic girl, my mother (Mary) tells me, unless they were hifalutin or Canadian in which case Marie was permissible. What knocks me out when I think of it is the overwhelming presumption of the working class, as well as their matter-of-fact faith. The girls who grow up beautiful and slender with what's known as "every opportunity" in the East 70s or in spiffy Soho lofts have trivial monickers, like Brooke or Kimberly; but hordes of poor dumpy overweight moms in housecoats and carcoats in Brooklyn name their daughters (who'll end up looking just like them) after the Mother of God. Not a bad idea, really; despite the jejune artistic renderings, there's nothing to suggest that the Virgin Mother herself wasn't fat and dumpy in some Galilean version of a housecoat after what theologians, sounding like General Haig, call "the Christ-event." I like the idea: peasant woman with a throaty voice, deep lines, deep laugh like Magnani or a healthier Viveca Lindfors; or maybe just a chubby pale old lady with bad eyesight saying "Hiya" to old friends at a funeral, decades after her co-starring role in Salvation History.

Psalm

Each year I forget the simple fact
that spring's new leaves are of a sickly
hue, Lord; not at all the strong dark
green in Wallace Nutting silver-prints
of my youth. You remember: the country
lane a dozen miles from Boston running
past a field where the amazing pink
of dogwood and white of apple blossom posed
against high summer verdure, dark and beckoning.
Not so the oak by yonder carriage-house.
Call that green? It's half yellow, and its bark
is gray, not brown — no, silver today.
Clouds behind the clouds behind the yellow
clouds upstage, and behind them all a vast
emptiness, if the naked eye can be
believed. It can't, as You and science teach.
Teenaged children throw a ball around the street,
speed it on its way with expletives, while pre-
schoolers with their stately gait have their
ball, too, this one phosphorescent in a tiny
hand, a place to focus in the changing light,
which doesn't fade, but shifts perspective,
like the slim retarded girl in the gray or silver
make-believe fur who waits each afternoon
on the stoop or corner for the kids who play ball
to walk past and smile. I'm waiting, too.
Like a Doberman longs for an enormous field
big enough to run across as hard and as far
as it can; like Mr. Ahmed longs for a prospective
buyer to walk in so he can unload the Arabia
Felix Restaurant and happily return to the stony
village whose photograph adorns his menu; like
a bourgeois idealist longs to see the world

through Wallace Nutting's eyes, in which
the chlorophyll does its job right; so my soul
longs for You, Lord, for the vast amused amazement
of your grace, in this your Strong (and holy) Place.

II.

The Morning

The vitamin-charged slush of Total cereal,
momentum of an early start,
the Breviary's poetry, a flash
of insight from the TV preacher who's dressed
in ever more appalling polyester suits . . .
I shun them. It's the morning,
all I care to know for its duration.
Dream of, of, of . . . can't recall, but
the night before I dreamt I was in bed with someone
I was gaga about. Woke up and there he was,
gaga in his sleep, moans, thrashing.
My nervous clients think I need a thrashing
—"On the stick, you!" — and they're right
on one level, theirs. A story up, I see
an old woman whose arms seem filled with slush
shouting from her window, like Molly Goldberg
on Fifties TV, and I wonder the same thing
I wondered as a tot about the home tube stars:
I see them through a glass, can they see me?
Appropriately darkly. Through the speakers
I learn what Pierre Boulez was getting at
in *Le Marteau sans Maitre*. Un question, Monsieur:
did your hammer demand emancipation
or had it always been a freelance tool?
I risk playing the fool
because this is a world I am creating,
not "text" or "slice of life," and old contexts
don't hold. "Water, water!" A parched prospector
crawls downhill toward the container port.
He plops into the harbor like a grizzled seal,
treads water and surveys the scene.
Stage left: bridges, helicopters overhead.
Stage right: the islands Puerto Rican couples

with tots and prams survey from Bay Ridge Park.
This world's finest anchorage is filled with freighters
which themselves are filled with freight
from everywhere. Drop it here. Then
back through the Narrows to the endless sea.

.

A Sense

of time present, in colors of the stone
and mortar of the houses built by times-
past generations on the street that I'm
traversing. I have made them each my own

in borrowed light of a midwinter sky,
midafternoon, as classes end and shouts
in timeless modes roll down the hill and out
into the harbor where they fade and die.

From my position, that's the way it seems,
Joralemon and Clinton, where St. Ann's
pink stone confection looks delicious, and
the eyes of wayward children fill my dreams

like crumbs for starlings threatened by the frost.
On their way homeward, watch them flick an ash,
the joint that hangs beneath a down moustache
a vehicle for downhill rides, to Lost

from Confident and Callow. It's a trip
I've taken, rider on a bumpy sledge,
whose mileage makes me think I have an edge,
"experience" that lets me let 'er rip

but don't — not even when compared to these,
the unbruised, unexamined of the day
who light up, deeply draw and drift away.
Each, walking past, provokes a little breeze

that fades like memories of being driven
by elders to the treeless city where
a "permanent" was something done to hair
and light the sum of all the time we're given.

The Nineteenth Century Is 183 Years Old

FOR KEITH MILOW

It creaks, that Saint-
Saens piece for the piano, grand
in its way, for its century,
which never seems to end: Camille,
1835 to eternity. In the icetray
of musical notation, Saint-Saens is
the cube with the favor frozen inside,
a scarab labeled "Hope" or "Despair," the invasion
of dinner by a horde of Euclidean forms.
They leave their laundry everywhere: their melody,
their progressive politics and chords, their timing
and their sense of time, their long line
to the bathroom and their dark forebodings
for this Administration and the next one,
dumped on the linoleum. A finger
pointed ceilingward for emphasis
can be pure gesture, but the vectors
proceeding from its tip are boring
a tunnel through your upstairs neighbor's
floor. Quiet down and listen to my gossip
about the dead. Saint-Saens liked to dress up
in women's clothes, that timeworn combination
of defiance and anxiety, evening gown and beard.
The bearded pianist Paul Jacobs told me that story.
He's dying of cancer, while the music
of this endless century persists.

Octavian

I had a point to make. Then I forgot it.
These days, to be "on" or "in" my mind's
a useless definition of a deep
half-truth. I was choked with rage. Then
I went to the seashore. Through the smoked
and non-prescription lenses, the stack of washed-
out primary tints shimmering with other-worldly
clarity from the parking lot beside the chowder
hut's a blowup of a science textbook graph,
"Alluvial Deposits": soft green of the beach
grass, toughest plant in America, laid beneath
the steel blue, then sea blue, then blue-
green of the ocean on the other side of which
you gambol, stripped into the composition
under a majolica sky. Colors from a Freilicher
or Porter, though I couldn't gauge the depth,
overlaid like drippings on the straw of a Chianti
bottle, the brand drunk exclusively by art school
sweethearts. At low tide, cast for sections
of our history to dredge up and resent, then
walked along the beach toward Wellfleet, practicing
my monologue. "I well remember the day
I thought it so unfair of you to gallivant
with young tarts on the further side of these
marine phenomena. It was yesterday, and as the last
light of evening found me on a spit between a tidal
swamp and the parapet of dunes that shields
the Herring Cove for spooners, I thought
you would deserve it if I turned to your bosom
friend, the one you made me promise never
under any circumstances to romance, and kissed him.
The fucking mosquitoes were impossible."
The newfound and regrettable tendency to turn

my life into an opera was washed out
by the colors for a blessed while. All that air
and a fluffy cloud that blocked the sun for half
an hour, as pettish as your coltish love
made me. I walked beneath the shadow of a deep
regret that such devout and histrionic passion
provoked no grand-scale tragedy, merely the usual
smorgasbord of bitterness and fantasies of murder
and revenge. Then the shadow lifted. I was on the quay
and you were on the packet leaving Illyria, clutching
the telegram that told you of your great-uncle's demise
and your whopping legacy. The wind blew your bangs back,
and the grimace never left your face as yell
after Confederate yell escaped your throat, progressively
overlaid by the thwack of waves as you shrank
to a speck above the boatwales, then disappeared.
There were postcards for awhile: "The Queen of the Nile
has a nice asp, har har. Miss you, X." That stripe.
After a delirious evening, I walked out with a roll
of silver to call you from the corner. It was snowing,
and the operator couldn't believe I had my forty
drachmas ready. Force-fed, the payphones in a five-
block radius died. Your voice had changed. I stopped
loving you and began to love the impossible, an image
of the two of us together. Then the libretto
shifted as the ingenue arrived onstage, and you
and I became a subplot in a farce of ancient
origin, though the music was ours. Eight
days a week, you know I really care. But gradually
one learns the impossibility of forcefeeding the time
that starts in pain as a tunnel, but opens
like a Chinese fingertrap with lack of strain
to reveal itself as the corkboard
on which the light one loves more than a lover
is tacked. I can spend all day here.
Then I'm going home to sleep. That's something
permanent, a concept more advanced than "final,"

which breaks down under the pressure
of knowing that it ends when you do, if
you do. The ocean shares the possibility as you
go deeper, until the dark line just below the sky
widens to another hue, one which can only
be imagined from here. There may be more,
and though there's not a drop to drink
in any of it, that's not why I came. I'm here
so the progressive fields of color are everything
between us. It was off the mark to call the fickle
boy Octavian, after the undergrad who changed
his name and filled his world with power.
And it was wrong to have given him a silver
rose, though it was an artful stratagem.
I wagered I could wrap the mutable
in immutable foil, but all I forged
was a gewgaw, fit for a suburban shelf
of Hummel figurines and family pix.
Today I picked a beach rose, which shriveled
at my touch. Then I pinned it to my bodice,
a spot of operatic sentiment to set against
the tempera of sea and sky, as packed
with light as ever, the greatest colors
for the emptiest parts of the world.

Four Organs

AFTER STEVE REICH

give the mind its head
in a choirloft when the spare beginnings
accordion and the harmonic
purr of a blower overlays the hit
or miss of a perfectionist on methedrine
which becomes a symphony of increments
unfollowable
but knowable in portions as the source
of pleasure as the wine flows
up the corkscrew
a process of intoxicating space
that grows to accommodate a wingspread
igniting the maracas
causing the whole to turn

Pretty Convincing

Talking to my friend Emily, whose drinking
patterns and extravagance of personal
feeling are a lot like mine, I'm pretty
convinced when she explains the things we do
while drinking (a cocktail to celebrate the new
account turns into a party that lasts till 3
a.m. and a terrific hangover) indicate
a problem of a sort I'd not considered.
I've been worried about how I metabolize
the sauce for four years, since my second bout
of hepatitis, when I kissed all the girls
at Christmas dinner and turned bright yellow
Christmas night, but never about whether
I could handle it. It's been more of a given,
the stage set for my life as an artistic queer,
as much of a tradition in these New York circles
as incense for Catholics or German
shepherds for the blind. We re-enact
the rituals, and our faces, like smoky icons
in a certain light, seem to learn nothing
but understand all. It comforts me
yet isn't all that pleasant, like drinking
Ripple to remember high school. A friend
of mine has been drinking in the same bar for decades,
talking to the same types, but progressively
fewer blonds. Joe LeSueur says he's glad
to have been a young man in the Fifties with his
Tab Hunter good looks, because that was the image
men desired; now it's the Puerto Rican
angel with great eyes and a fierce fidelity
that springs out of machismo, rather than a moral
choice. His argument is pretty convincing, too,
except lots of the pretty blonds I've known

default by dying young, leaving the field
to the swarthy. Cameron Burke, the dancer
and waiter at Magoo's, killed on his way home from
the Pines when a car hit his bike on the Sunrise Highway.
Henry Post dead of AIDS, a man I thought would be around
forever, surprising me by his mortality the way
I was surprised when I heard he was not
the grandson of Emily Post at all, just pretending,
like the friend he wrote about in *Playgirl*, Blair Meehan,
was faking when he crashed every A List party for a year
by pretending to be Kay Meehan's son, a masquerade
that ended when a hostess told him "Your mother's here"
and led him by the hand to the dowager —Woman, behold
thy son — underneath a darkening conviction that all,
if not wrong, was not right. By now Henry may have faced
the same embarrassment at some cocktail party in the sky.
Stay as outrageously nasty as you were. And Patrick
Mack, locked into my memory as he held court in the Anvil
by the downstairs pinball machine, and writhing
as he danced in Lita Hornick's parlor when the Stimulators
played her party, dead last week of causes I don't know,
as if the cause and not the effect were the problem.
My blond friend Chuck Shaw refers to the Bone-
crusher in the Sky, and I'm starting to
imagine a road to his castle lit by radiant
heads of blonds on poles as streetlamps for the gods,
flickering on at twilight as I used to do
in the years when I crashed more parties and acted
more outrageously and met more beauties and made
more enemies than ever before or ever again, I pray.
It's spring and there's another crop of kids
with haircuts from my childhood and inflated self-esteem
from my arrival in New York, who plug into the history
of prettiness, convincing to themselves and the devout.
We who are about to catch the eye of someone
new salute as the cotillion passes, led by blonds
and followed by the rest of us, a formal march

to the dark edge of the ballroom where we step out
onto the terrace and the buds on the forsythia
that hides the trash sprout magically
at our approach. I toast it
as memorial to dreams as fragile and persistent
as a blond in love. My clothes smell like the smoky
bar, but the sweetness of the April air's
delicious when I step outside and fill
my lungs, leaning my head back
in a first-class seat on the shuttle
between the rowdy celebration of great deeds
to come and an enormous Irish wake in which
the corpses change but the party goes on forever.

This Much Fun

HEAVEN IS A PLACE WHERE NOTHING EVER HAPPENS.
                                              DAVID BYRNE

Poised as if to fly, the sea-
bird arches what will be its haunches
in a million years. The cable
flashes 'cross the Great Atlantic
and turns my chest to mush. No
birds on the cables of the Brooklyn
Bridge — too noisy — but the view
I step into like blocking someone's telescope,
the dime-a-peep variety, 's as sweeping
as a Cinerama travelogue or diorama
battlefield or episode from Mormon history.
"Like a movie on TV" is how the boy
who saw his teacher shoot himself in class
described it. The cycles of these days
and nights reflected in the *TV Guide*'s
a kind of Daily Office: Matins,
I Love Lucy; *Dream House*, Lauds;
Love Boat as the liturgy for noon, then *Gilligan's
Island* speeds us toward the vesper light.
Something in the air that shimmers in the dawn's
damp blue seems kind by sunset; pathetic
and fallacious, too, but with all the best
intentions. There are ways of blocking out
the sound, and Collects for the major feasts:
the Birth of Little Ricky, or the loud arrival
from heaven of an astronaut, confused among
these puny castaways. I cast away my fear
of walking down the street with headphones
and tune in. "Good Friday Spell" from *Parsifal*
informs the G.E. Building's sunlit
spire, and "Fanfare for the Common Man"'s
a sweet reminder of revolutions lost on C.P.S.

To be this young and having this much
fun's a situation that makes me
nothing if not grateful. Some choice.
But glimmering in the distance is the forge
where somebody somebody used to love turns youth
into a weapon. I want to be nowhere
in that vicinity, a place that doesn't
exist because the qualities that put it on the map
of language come together only once, for all
of time, anonymous as the light
and secret as the air that it impregnates
in the smuggler's harbor. What's inside
the carton marked "Bananas" is the captain's
beeswax, not yours. But what's inside
the history is something over which you exercise
complete control. What's inside the feeling
is a range of permutations comfy by now,
the carburetor settings for the formal play
of light on architecture. Surfaces abound, but
translate into energy when you add a drop of language.
Things fall away, in other words, like scales
from the sides of fish who find their patch
of green-gray lousy with chemistry, though
one must admit it's an impressive river.
They wash up at our feet, lavabo
towels in fins. We thought they had to
swim, but they aspire to fly away the way
birds have to. I'm waiting for the milky
patches in my history to dry, sprout
feathers. I'm gonna love that man
till I die, a hypothetical
event beyond my ken. It happens
every day on the detective show
at twilight: a murder in the first
five minutes, a second halfway down
the plot line, to shut up a villain
pestered by scruples. It broadcasts

afternoons like clockwork, the kind
you never need to bother winding. When I feel
rundown, I think of daily horrors like that,
soothing not because of their dramatic
tension, but as demarcations of the antinomic
light that's always new, always familiar.
It's the same time it was yesterday
at this time, which makes me think of heaven,
and hell, too, both of which may boil
down to the same thing finally: a place
filled up with more than you can know
or handle, whose limits are your own
and whose events are functions of those limits;
I'm half-blind. There's no getting out of it,
anymore than out of this frenetic day,
whose edges have been planed by the triumphal
music, a perfect reason for tuning it in,
but not for writing it down or thinking
it can really help. Nothing can. But nothing's
all I pack these days on long trips
through the daylight, as new as forms that we
extrapolate then shatter, as empty
as the forms to come and the amazing energy
that shoots through and illuminates their most
apparent qualities. It keeps me going
in circles that constitute a tour
of the horizon, as far as I can see
or ever will, when "ever" means "today."

III.

King of the Wood

Know you not
your father's house and name?
We were driving up Mulholland,
my Dad and I, a month or so
ago, in the big white Ford
with which I'd passed my road test.
Speedometers back then went up as far
as one-eighty, two hundred even,
even though anything out of Detroit
would fall apart if driven half that fast.
I asked my Dad, "What is it like to die?"
He paused, gave me a withering look,
and said, "It's not *like* anything."

Later we were separated. Always
it's that way near the end of the dream:
a landslide blocks the trail down which I've walked
for gasoline in an old-fashioned can;
a cable snaps. Trying to circle
round the long way, I stumble down
the steep hill toward the stream.
My friends have just untied their raft.
They float away and wave, "Moon River"
up and over. Where have they gone?
Kennst du das Land?

I lived there for a long time.
I remember best the woods
behind the house, and what we built there,
forts, traps, rungs nailed to the side
of an enormous spruce by boys
so long ago we didn't know their names.
They'd fought in the war.

There was a boy in the class, the store,
the magazine I didn't like.
Then after awhile I liked him.
Awhile more, and I'll like him more or less
the same, or more, or less.
It's happened enough times for me to know
what's coming: not a pattern
exactly, for it's always different;
more a vehicle that you can climb
inside at any point. You can leave, too,
but it will be the hardest thing you ever did.
You've gotten used to seeing it one way,
and who's to tell you you're not right?
"A painter sees a hairbrush in the butter, and to him
it's all reflected light." Virgil said that,
Virgil Thomson. Later the same night,
he made the rounds among his guests,
a wicker basket filled with withered pears
hanging from his hands, and squeaked,
"The harder they are, the better they taste."

In which meaning is a quantity,
a participle, meaning that the range
of permutations in a band of time
is evened out and frozen, life the plinth
for ice sculptures of growing love, abiding
love, and the collapse of love through perfidy
or blind neglect   in which the moment is
the only one there is   a day at a time
is too long   have a second, then another
second   ragged men in elephant bells
in a meeting room on St. Mark's Place
holding off another bottle for another
moment   you've had a successful moment,
the only one there is, the point
at which the denouement's epitomized
in stylized gestures, when the whole ballet
depends on how it looks, which hinges
on the way it feels, its definition
like good cheekbones, their quality obvious
enough to make you first a movie star
and then a princess   you never dreamed
you'd get that far, but then you never thought
you'd have gotten this far, either

in which you share a common symbol
for each thing, and wouldn't know
the thing at all without its symbol
a city of amnesiacs who paste
the names of objects on the things themselves
to start a hundred years of solitude   anything
can happen here, and anything does
the freedom of the moment is the freedom
of the aquarium, the gay ceramic
turrets of the castle through whose windows
goldfish swim a blur
behind the glass that buttresses their world
outside the window, fish food falls,

settling on the sills like snow
if you were an Eskimo, you could call it one
of twenty names, depending on the way
it looked, a notion of abundance
determined by the names one knows
I've died a thousand deaths, a wealth of deaths,
while waiting for you here   I was afraid
that something might have happened to you, something
terrible   and that you wouldn't come

in which you find it easy, almost glib,
to marshal forces and to summon up
the feelings and the memories for the sake
of structures you would sometimes rather torch:
the mediocre bandshell, or the pavilion
with broken steps and vulgar sentiments
carved into the crossbeams by a hundred years
of self-important boys with knives
this was their place, and you'd just as soon
send the whole thing up in smoke
first the planks   then the walls that arch
around the windows   then the roof   then
the trees and the whole wood   then the lake
then the air   then the earth
but not the way you'll talk about it later

in which the blackened husk contains the seeds
of everything you burnt away, grown back
when another moment's light expels
the dark your eyelids buttressed in your eyes
not a thing has changed, only its significance
the way a drawing by a genius when erased
by another genius is another work of art,
completely new   if not a world, its map

Night goes up in . . . smoke? No, fog.
A. C sharp. C sharp. A. G.
Foghorn into symphony
needs another medium

than the words with which I make
my art. Wagner comes to mind,
the insufficiency of line . . .
leitmotivs to light the depths.

Scientific instruments,
aimed precisely at the ships,
map them out as little blips,
but could never catch the rays

jaundiced through a hangdog mist,
tumbling wisps that dramatize
thin beams that will energize
them away in minutes now.

As the planet warms, I heat
coffee the ten-thousandth time.
Words, alas, aren't music. I'm
glad to be here all the same.

Go gently into that good morning,
Go gently into that good day.
Don't leave a trace behind
of the love that you will find.
You've got more good reasons for leaving, boy,
than to stay.

Peter, Paul and Mary sang that to me in a dream
when I was sixteen. It's stayed with me.
Later on, it made me feel a kin
of Jeanne D'Arc. Somebody was calling,
somebody I couldn't see. I didn't know
the voices, but I could tell that they
were strong. I thought of stripping off
the clothes my father bought me, standing
naked in the style of Francis ("free"),
my father's patron saint and mine.
I'd wanted other-worldly intervention
for so long, the angel
who'd tell me there had been a terrible
mistake, my fortune and my father
were in another place, please follow . . .

In all the places where I've spent
the moments, I've known it was my song.
How could I be sure?
In a world that's constantly changing,
how could I be sure?

I feel it. I feel it
in my bones.

O say, can you see?
Jess, I can see very well. And the Mexican
waved from the top of the ballpark flagpole.
That's a joke, son. I turned on the cartoons
to turn him off. Has anybody here seen my old
friend Kelly with the Irish eyes?
He's as bad as old Antonio. 200 pounds
of twisted steel and sex appeal. You'd never
believe it, but your father was thin
when I married him. And light on his feet.
There's a painting of the major transportation systems
outside a Southern or a Western city
breaking down — planes crashing, station wagons
hurtling toward the ditch — and the souls
of passengers ascending light as fog
into the air. They're
wearing long white robes, like Klansmen
or the children visited by Peter Pan.
I never wanted to grow up and be
like he was, and now I haven't.

Fresh as red air of Tuscany, the dawn
of the twelfth-century Renaissance, a dry
run for the full-blown windstorm, centuries down

the rough track from Firenze, he would be
of countenance. Something Frank there, Frankish as his
    name,
a monicker brought back from shopping sprees

by nouveau-riches embarrassing parents,
the Bernadones, merchants to grandees,
mongers of cloth for vestments

exquisite as smoky parades of preening
clerks whose every gesture rubrics mapped,
whose purses turned to pouts when students leaning

in doorways hurled processionward their japes,
sparking absurd exchanges: "Prig!" "Young lout!"
"Old queen!" "Barbarian!" "Fatso!" "Jackanapes!"

My namesake jeered the loudest, irresponsible
and drop-dead charming as I might have seemed
in my best moments, halfway through a full

tumbler of Scotch (my second), two away
from that blissful, combustible insouciance
when anything — a gaffe, a gorgeous lay,

the loss of friends — was possible, and came
to pass more often as I passed the blacked-
out bulb that marked my limit, or in flames

passed out. Francis passed out through the city gates.
He knew of nothing worthwhile that he lacked —
top school, designer threads, a string of dates,

with sylphs — but someone older, wise and still,
a father-figure to replace the hair-
trigger-tempered draper, and to fill

the space left by his fawning. In the wood
he stumbled down a stony path to where
the tumbledown San Damiano stood,

a broken chapel. Then a sudden lurch,
as if sodden or uncertain of foot
when someone's voice said, "Build my church."

He raised it stone on stone, as troubadours
build words on music, probably employing
conventions in inverted commas, new or

clever usages for timeworn slabs
of hewn granite, repairing cracks,
painstaking as, home from his cluttered lab,

a chemist builds a fireplace brick by brick in
the cleared thicket between lawn and wood,
my father in the summer half-light, kneeling

with trowel and barrow.
He used it to burn trash
when he finished it. I don't know

how Francis used St. D's. His days were full
of roles: jongleur de Dieu, gentle seafarer
to sultanates, ambassador to wolves,

finally living like one, in a stinking
cave, the native freshness drained
out of his narrow face into the sinking

hollows of his eyes, like classic form
drained of all referents but a multitude
of fashions through the years, or men in uniform

of burnt sienna sack,
museum keepers of the holy sites
of history, builders of shrines to way-back-

when phenomena, his life's blood leaching
out of his wrists into black Umbrian soil
as if an I.V. had been yanked, and reaching

past swarms of sounds for the right words,
the ones he'd heard once only, his ears
large for them as a spindly deer's. I heard

a voice, know the words it used,
but did I get my father's meaning right?
All of it gets confused

except the question, beaten half to death,
a swarm of bees that chase a fat-legged toddler
all the way home, a temple out of breath.

To Walter Lowenfels

You had four real ones of your own, so why
did you write *To an Imaginary
Daughter*? I found it in the Books
for a Buck bin at Barnes & Noble,
your signature inside, a copy you'd inscribed
to someone whom you'd just rejected
for one of your anthologies of wooly
Movement writing, to which you gave your life
in language of your time, the Great Depression.
It's depressing how unrecognizable
your name's become; with Hemingway and
Henry Miller, one of the three
most prominent and best expatriate
writers in Paris; author of *Steel*,
the pamphlet that made bosses of the day
see Red. Your popularity
like vaunted winds of change, swept through
the corners of the world lit by Left-Lit
and out the window, like the wind today
that drove me into Barnes & Noble.
It's cold out there when no one knows
your name. Spokesman, working-class
Whitmanic bard, poet of the brave
new world, speaker of demotic
democratic truths, mover and shaker, shock-troop
of the Revolution, too-accessible
parent of forgotten books: I know your slim
affected and affecting offspring
only because some miffed, less-than-forgotten
scribbler sold it off for change.
The verdict of the History you used
as engine and excuse is not in yet,
you'd say. I'll stick around.
But I'm haunted by the lack of rhyme
and reason in how power dwindles down

---

from clarity and massive sweep
of language to a garrulous old man
in Peekskill serving French bread and Bordeaux
to luncheon guests. "He wore a black beret;
the old days were important to him."

Father of vanished texts, where went your truth?
The wind has cleared away your agitprop,
your art, your bromides, your imaginings
of world, or word, or children strong of grip
enough to clasp, to spare your voice.

Hercules becomes Celestial
Hercules. The son whose flesh
is eaten by the faithful once a year,
stripped from his bones, his bones
burnt, his ashes smeared across their brows,
grows slowly brighter through the centuries
and rises skyward, Sonny to sun.
Some of the farflung 'burbs confused him
with Apollo — bright chariot in the air,
flames painted on the side, chrome trim, and Steve
Reeves driving, as in "Hercules Unchained"
(the farts-and-popcorn-on-a-rainy-day
smell of the Majestic Theater, where
the picture filled the house . . . how did he make
his pecs so shiny?) Think of all that beef
whetting the most private imaginings
of throngs of kids who walked out blinking
at the strong sunlight which had changed the sky
outdoors while they were helping Joe Levine
stay rich. It's a rich life
when you stop being a host or victim
and when your mother no longer can tell you
what to do — feed the guests, son —
and your father hands you a piece of the family
business, till the day he leaves
to be much spoken of, but never seen
and there you are at the reins, waving
at the kids you shared a movie with
a long time ago, as you pass the stretch
of wood and head toward Westfield. Getting older
isn't what you thought; it's gradual
and pleasant, and has something to do
with healing, the way a cut dries up
and closes on its own, with time.
Hercules was interchangeable
with Aesculapius, once he began
his journey to the sky, taking over

where the old king left off, trajectory
predictable as missiles homing in,
a notion indicating that a home
presents itself at some point down the trail,
though present time seems not to hold it, just
the intimation of a happy splashdown
and the start of one more orbit, another day
filled to the brim with light.

Exult now, all you angels and archangels,
You citizens of heaven and of Cobble Hill,
Who touch a spark to tinder in a Webber grill
And sprinkle points of light from taper

To slender candles trembling in the knobby fists
Of old woman and callow teen
And all the ages in between
The nervous shadows on their faces veiled in mist

Of incense and the ancient import
Of texts announcing someone risen for their sake
Ejected from a tomb at daybreak
The planet his new mother, on his way to short

And mystifying conversations
With friends before departing for his Father's side
A presence in the world, as though he never died
Coloring the darkness with anticipation

Together with the smoke and tapers
It brings to mind a hillside on a summer night
When "We Shall Overcome" by torchlight
Projected from a thousand throats, across the acres

Of tombstones for the war dead, more dead
Each day across the ocean, and a man who'd tried
To stop the killing but had died
Before he had the chance, planted among them

We waited for his wife and children
The Cardinal Archbishop said a hurried Mass
And from an altar torch a fragile flame was passed
Out to the candles held by adolescent pilgrims

Whose reedy song was drowned by jet noise
Of aircraft dropping from the sky like burning gel
To land a mile away, at National
Where at the runway's end my father closed his eyes

His earphone in, relaxing in the Ford
And listening to pilot-tower
Communications by the hour
He'd sit all evening that way, never growing bored

I passed the flame to Jack O'Hara
He passed it to a monk in casual attire
In the confusion, Judy Jenkins' hair caught fire
We smothered it, and smothered laughter

Solemnity derailed by sudden fright
As some creep with a pistol had derailed our dreams
For darkness can hold anything, although it seems
to dissipate so easily for candlelight

In this dimly lit place, dim hour
We raise our voices and our song
We'd thought him dead, but were dead wrong
He's risen as he said, with endless grace and power

Where Is Art?

Georgia Brown in a dingy
period costume in a dingy
Soho room in a faded
photo of a Broadway stage,
asking in a melody
in a rhyme on a scratchy
LP, Where is what she cares
about the most, and it's the first
image that springs (spring
forward, fall back) into my mind
when I wonder, where is what
I used to care about the most,
the art of it, not artifice
like sweeteners I despise
but a thing I cared about,
care about losing touch with
enough that when the adjective
"artful" provokes an unsavory
image (Artful Dodger) I wonder
if that's the kind of art I was
making all along, clever and evasive,
like framing the question in lines
that fit too easily into what appears
to be a poem, as if to write it
that way were enough, when what
it needed was philosophy, the love
of wisdom (Where is love?) and something
behind the words when emptiness begins
to pass as profundity, to fill up
the heart when a dearth of energy
starts to pass as openness to life
and I'm running on nerves alone
and I think that's "romantic," compounding
the vulgar interest in a cheap facade

there is language behind whose clarity
stands the masterpiece that Malevich
never got around to painting   and
there is the rococo church behind
which is all the alcohol and caffeine
of the past ten years

Old man, look at my life
thirty-five and still alive   apart
from that we're more alike
every time I look   I'm
learning that the edge of night
is not the brink the starved
coyote tumbles from in his compulsive
hunt for an elusive fowl
in Saturday cartoons   nor do
I want to think the night so huge
as to resemble those sheer canyons
down which the coyote falls
to splatter with a sound
unheard by the above-it-all
observer, who notes how insignificant
such pain and disappointment seem
in this vast landscape   I want
to see the night as where the glow
thrown out by the campfire stops
and see the light as gravity
drawing the annoying creatures
of the wood as near its heart
as they can bear   where
absence is a hole chewed in a garment
by the ones we find it inconvenient
to have around   and every feeling
from exhilaration to a sense
of loss begins with intimations
that the borders which define the homely
and the unfamiliar always fray
the way that constellations draw the eye
to where the light has punched
its way into the squares of darkness
outside the windows of a lighted room

October

FOR DUNCAN HANNAH

An afternoon of steady light
That clears the air, and clearly shows
Each imperfection in the skin,
Each gap within the ragged rows

Of stalks and dusty gleanings left
When crops were harvested and sent
To cities where the people shop
For seasoning, for nourishment.

As though lit from within, the strips
Of earth across the gentle hill
Glow with the fiery colors of
The dying leaves, or, fiercer still,

Are shadowed by the sleeping vines
That stiffly curl and seem to die,
And on a cart, someone to watch
The empty fields, the empty sky.

Dear heart, wish you or I were here or there . . .
No. That's not true.
I wish I knew that you
were happy now, and sure at last
of being loved. I loved
our long talks late at night
when all the others were in bed. We'd fight
about the war and Watergate, and sip
Virginia Gentleman (one was your limit).
Your image doesn't dim; it
resonates through all my life.
So many times I've wanted
to call you up or walk downstairs
to your domain, the basement
with its toolbench and pine-paneled
walls, you in a dark mood slouching
over your ham radio, to coax you
back into the light, make you laugh.
Above my desk I have the photograph
of you kneeling beside me in the garden
that the wood absorbed. I'm two and nervous
in the little plastic pool. You're
having a good time with your Number One Son,
smiling more broadly than I can recall
outside of snapshots, though I can remember all
your other faces: stolid in the pew
at church, sublime intentness of a natural
engineer at your electric saw, or soldering
a new attachment to the jerrybuilt
shortwave, red with fury
over being baited or some imaginary
provocation, but mostly
when someone didn't listen.
I see your face the times I wasn't there,
as well: weeping to me on the phone
about the total failure of your life
for a good two hours (I couldn't

decide if you were going bonkers or having
a Pascal-like moment of clear light),
or how you looked the night
of your attack, feeling it come
over you as Ted Koppel asked pithy questions
on the little screen, unable to call out
in answer or for help. I've learned
the difference between a silence
and an absence since your quick
departure. There's no "where"
there, wherever you are. When I talk
to you these days, I end up trying
to convince myself that I'm pretending,
and failing to. It makes me think of you
tapping out a signal like a blind man
on your Morse code key, to strangers
who could understand the special
language that you used, projecting it
along a wire from underground
into the air, into the world.

IV.

Cape and Islands

Little birdie footprints. Then a rush
of gray surf ridden by the yellow smut
of brine or soapsuds flushed by visitors
from off-island, down to the sea. It bastes
the sand in preparation for a meal
the ocean takes in small bites, pecking
like a bird. The surgical acuity of morning
light's sharp angle dapples fish
who opened wide to feast on visitors
from neighboring dominions, and were yanked
from theirs. The birds race the waves back out,
scouting dross for something edible. Whoosh.
There go their footprints again. The edges of a time
make birds and sea take turns, the way the edges
of a space stove in the bottom
of my ship and keep me from traversing
that stretch of sea. "Web of life" and "fabric
of time" denote a single skein: the third
dimension of the dotted line on the map
between your life and theirs. You can't
get there from here; what seems like a wall
of windows is the net itself.
No place is not an island or a detail
of one: not this frangible
ping-pong ball of a planet, its lagoon-
before-the-electric-storm watercolors ridden
by white smut, disassembling
and reforming in patterns of a delicacy
and votive or other scientific significance
that might be intentional, a signal
we have not yet grasped; not the mass
of land, no longer continent, coloring
the ocean twenty miles away with sludge;

not the lonely town, whose lights are less
a scalpel in the night than a suspension
which becomes a sediment the closer to
the cottage it gets. Places at the bottom
of the sky, a continuum
like human skin, no less surrounded
because one can never find the edge one needs
for peeling off the mudpack or harvesting
the morning crop of beard. The Razor-
backs, the Jets, the Terrapins, the Knights:
armies 'neath the lights
whose ignorance is bald or receding like the dunes
of Coast Guard Beach, the gums of America. The Crimson
Tide swoops into the bay and sticks around like smut,
crusting and intoxicating clams. There is a blight
in the affairs of men, as tangible
as gooseflesh to the blind, who provoke it
through no fault of their own. They're alone
in a world of perpetual darkness. Across
the border is another state, from which the sound
of foreign words in delicate incomprehensible
patterns caroms back. They're playing
ping-pong over there, having a wonderful time.
Together we have formed a union, though drastically alop
to visitors with the rudest social sense: "The Heiress
and the Waiter," "The Shiftless Boy and the Adoring
Priest." We're looking for a sort of stability
which depends on absence. The blind lead the mapless,
and though they're sure of foot along
the causeway through the bog, there's no way
they can know the charm and endless
pain and entertainment of the disconnected
sectors of the city where their voyage ends.
From the plane, a sky the optimistic
color of the UN flag gives way to shades
of green, green smut. They're near the airport.
All it takes to bridge the physical

distance is a little hop across the weather
or its absence, but to stitch the sense
of placement in the center of a field
of vision to the rattletrap conventions
out of which you live as from a weekend bag
requires a vehicle: a football
that rotates on its axis, shaking off
the cartoon fleas as it heads for your solar
plexus at the speed of sound. Someone
threw that thing at you, and wants you
to run with it, not fumble; but to where?
Even the biggest voice across the widest stage
booming out to the largest audience
in history can't solve the problem
of what to do with all that space
between the words, the proof that there is more
to come, something that you haven't heard
which will teach you more about the place
you see or the places you have learned about
from previous communiqués. They require an answer.
I have a hard time sometimes thinking
I am really here. The lady in the bar
with the wig teased into a ski-slope
ending at a precipice of forehead and a massive
chin could not be Ethel Merman, no matter
how alike they looked. Maybe I thought
it was impossible because it was me
this was happening to. Now that she's dead,
I'd think it was especially impossible, but maybe
there's a place where it could still be Ethel
Merman at the bar. Maybe my perception of the boundary
around this island is as weak as it was
that night, and the range of communiqués
is greater than I'd ever dream. At the foot
of the street is a river. You'd never dream
a tunnel with a train was far beneath it
unless you knew, a knowledge that depends

on people other than you. Once across the river,
another foot of another street dead-ends
at another, larger river, under which
a train runs, too. Hey. Hey, it's me.
It's what you want to shout into the sky
when the last sad traces of pastel
fade into the twilight zone of steeples
and green docks on the far side of the water.
In the Lower Bay, what appears a mothball fleet
has people on its decks when seen through Dad's
binoculars. They're playing ping-pong
or football in an easy give-and-take,
the principle behind their action not unlike
the way you breathe, or have to figure out
what something someone says really means.
The air turns frigid instantly, and it's time
to go beneath the water on a train
and run into the people whom you say
you know while doubting it, although
you never can be sure they're not exactly
what you think they are, the way the woman
in the bar turned out to be Ethel Merman.
She opened her mouth and in an unmistakable
voice said, "Vodka and orange juice, Eddie,"
a sentiment I've echoed hundreds of times
in the intervening years. A votive
current runs beneath the pleasantries.
You watch it as it turns into a sewer
of the histories, yours and the ones
you catch, like viruses or lower forms
of sealife to voracious birds. I'm nesting here
in the remnants of the gifts that washed up
after the storm. I cannot be anything
but grateful, though I aspire to be,
the way that burly seamen round the Horn
and aspire to home, a cozy port that starts
to exist when they lose sight of land.

I'd never been that far away before, and I needed
something to connect me to the places
that I knew, a rope or language. We're going
to sell what we have, then we're going
to buy new things, and we'll be back before
you know it, to bring them to your little nests.
I can see the harbor beacon now,
and the pelicans, the gargoyle
guardians of the green pier's uprights.
We stepped ashore at sunset, to the cheers
of a throng in motley: bongo
drummers, the Iguana Man, a clutch
of Ethel Merman lookalikes, and boys
whose skins seemed burnished, then buffed.
Every man should have an adventure like that.
They mistook our "hallos" for "aloes,"
a plant of strong medicinal
properties they grow. With delicate
incomprehensible gestures they led us
down a causeway to the aloe bogs,
past shabby bungalows, each rooftop crowned
with wheels for nesting storks.
We learned through observation that the crowd
of well-wishers at our sloop's arrival
had turned out not to greet us, but to say
Goodbye to the sun, and that they gathered
thus each afternoon. In my years among them,
I learned many secrets: skin care, bongo
drumming, and darker ones of which I may not speak.
I met a burnished maiden there, and married her.
She is your mother. But something alien
persisted, even in the heat
of sex in the horse latitudes or trying to speak
the inutterable in a tongue
I barely understood. A subtext
lay beneath the coral and the sand
like a water table when the kitchen tap

is clogged. Millions live that way, trudging miles
up mountainsides on stony paths to springs,
to lug back dippersful in tall ceramic
jars their culture's lost the knack of making,
relics from the days before the well
their grandfathers dug ran dry.
We're getting farther from the source
of our predicament, which led us to the birth
of narrative. But sequence is as much
an artifice as the perfectly preserved
seaside village where you brought your family
on your return. Those people are nothing
like their forebears; rather, there's no way you can know.
I thought I knew this person, and that we
were friends; then he did something
terrible, incredibly mean. Maybe
I never knew him. Maybe he was not the same
person I knew. I told him
all my secrets, even the dark ones.
Now the knowledge lies behind
his gestures, as familiar as the light
that floods the shed where we put up preserves.
What he does with it's his own
business. The ball's in his court.
I'm getting thirsty waiting for the serve.
It's one of those spaces, where the sluggish
pace slows down the asymptotic
progress of the game. There's just the light
and the knowledge of your own heart
at work, not the things that fill it
but the way it moves. A Valentine
is etched upon a chamber wall. The millrace
of your blood washes it away. Whoosh.
The shards are off on an excursion
down your body's highways, to return unrecognizable.
I was afraid you wouldn't recognize me,
so I tried to stay the same, but pressure

built up like a boil that festered
despite my expertise in skin care, an oubliette
of smut churned up by history
I tried to trap. That's when I went to the beach.
The air looks non-existent here, though
I feel it on my skin. The sandpipers' strategy
vis-a-vis the waves persists: quick bite,
quick flight, repeated as the day
grows logy and the shadows corpulent.
I have a hard time sometimes remembering
I'm part of the largest audience watching
as the largest stage in history is trod
by those unfolding a sequence that at first
seems tawdry. The nightclub owner and his fleshy
love walk out along the moonlit seawall.
The song they sing in their loudest voices
is kitsch, and their lines predictable. Yet
the clumsy hand of one barely encircles
the other's waist at the end
of the number, as if frightened
by what it will or won't discover.
In a dream, the gesture stopped the show;
like falling down a stairwell or an empty
shaft of light, the incompletion
and its resultant terror woke you up.
A motion out of time, and a voice to say
it's time and you're almost out of it. But
gradually that shipwrecked feeling yields
to a nascent certitude, the edges of which
won't take shape, like batter that resists
the form you need for breakfast, spreading out
to form a layer of porous comprehension
across the horizonless stretch
of darkness when the noises of the waves
blot out the thoughts you live by, or try to.
It's not that something's missing; it's simply
that the colors haven't filled the spaces

in yet. It's a project, like fishing,
to stitch a half-completed history
out of whole cloth. I stayed in Key West
for awhile. Then I went to Broadway to audition
for a leading role. I fell in with the nephew
of a famous writer, then split for Mykonos
to cool it out. Once there, I rooted
for my favorite teams: the Bright Eyes, the Poltroons,
the Vipers with the Best Intentions, and the white
stucco walls of individual
houses which have stood in the same place
forever, islands in the muddy
tidal flat of time on an island
where all the time in the world is receding
like the dream which, for once,
gave you all the clues you needed
to plug the hull and plot the course
back to your island home.

The Fruit Streets

There's a little cottage in the back
of a composed facade. I want
to live there. There's a little
composition I can doodle on the keys
in basic chords. The man with an electric
speaker where his voice should be
in corduroy is sweeping down
the Fruit Streets, as a lady
inside my cloudy memory of other lives
or movies sweeps the cobblestones
with her train. She's on her way
to Pilgrim Church, where Beecher thunders.
Rain sweeps in from the bay.
I wonder how much good a sermon
can do, though they were once as popular
as cautionary soaps about the rich
to rubes today. Within the stiffness
of a form and collar let me touch
your eyes, take your hand. I'll lead you
to a land of colors — Cranberry, Pineapple,
Orange and the spurious Joralemon — and thrilling
tastes. The rawness of the wind is softened
by a blast of citrus, as the view
from the Heights gains pigment with a flick
of the Tint dial. It's a new world
out there, as if a box of Trix
had spilled across the harbor where the grays
and silvers played beneath a sky they perfectly
resembled. In the glow of an ass-backwards
native lore, Paradise could be as sudden
as a bite of fruit, or death
to the congregants. Protestants
find both "forbidden," though the preacher

whose words moved a government himself
may have brewed the metaphor while doodling
with a colleague's wife. The life
of the flesh is lived inside a sack
of flesh, but the life of the memory
is spun out in the names by which
we know the streets. It was here
I smoked a joint with John before he left
to turn into a rock star on the Coast
and watched the fireworks.
They lit up the sky,
Cranberry red, Pineapple yellow,
Orange orange, against the electric
blue-engorged horizon, radiant scrim
you can point to any twilight on your way
to drinks with friends, silly rabbits.
Pellets of our histories have piled up
in my mind, the Nation's Attic,
a nation carried onward by the names
of streets and Protestants like Carrie Nation,
where hatchets that remain unburied
reduce saloons to slivers. There's a beam
of pale light playing on a chink between
the landmark's bricks, a sliver of decay.
It's colorless, a paradigm of how I want to look
to let you see through what I say to find
the cottage with the patch of lawn where I live,
a dooryard in the patchwork of a city
you know about because you've heard it
in my voice, as if by faith.

Desire Under the Pines

I like to wake up early by myself
and walk out to the forest which divides
the beach from bay side of the island, like
the line of hair that starts at breastbone, hides

the navel and descends into the thatch
beneath the tan line of a boy I saw
a picture of once, in a magazine.
He isn't in the woods this morning. Raw

desire al fresco isn't quite my speed
these months. I like to scout for vireos
and robins almost as much as for guys.
An ashtray from the Hotel Timeo

in Taormina, a signed lithograph
by the late Tony Smith, and a shelf packed
with great books of our time: the souvenirs
of my hosts' histories. I left mine back

along the trail, like interesting litter
thrown out of Conestogas on the long
trek west. The drivers knew that "We can use it
in Oregon" was a completely wrong

criterion. They had to get there first,
and lightening the load was the only way.
Beside the path, the wren that lights in brush
sounds like a footstep in the gathering day.

Lit

As if the light contained an outer room
and secret inner chamber which initiates
could enter through the door of the grandfather
clock's dark case, lowering the weights
and pendulum to work the silent
gears and swing a boy-sized square
of wainscoting aside, exposing the hatch
to the hideaway of the richest man
in America, which overlaps the setting
of your life the way competing theories
of light complete each other's mysteries,
by cancelling the possibility that either could be
wholly right, or like the surface of the bay
on a particular breezy day, the one in which
you scarred your thigh on the towline, taking you
off skis, out of the sun. When you came
to the city, you wished you had a deeper tan.
I'm here to help you lower that desire
from your bike to the Sheep Meadow's waves,
perceptible from just one angle, of crewcut
green so uniform it might have been applied
in a single stroke with the broadest brush,
or for another reason.

Words For Simone Weil

attention, it is a poem
but uncomposed, the way a fearsome sky
shakes out its skirts attempting to decide
to rain on them, handing the pathos back

the fallacy: desire exists outside
the closed world of a chest whose ardent heaves
don't rustle its own lining of dead leaves
a Petri dish, a common meal, a bone

one thing to chew on, something else to know
it's yours to eat before you eat it   best
to save it, not a torture, not a test
a tension, like a poem you can watch

obedient to the movement and the whole
of a vast midland, all you ever see
the brown and yellow clouds mean history
for now, for then, for when you heed them both

July

FOR DARRAGH PARK

THE FOOT SHOULD NEVER GO WHERE THE EYE HAS ALREADY BEEN.
                                        CAPABILITY BROWN

I knew the place had capabilities
the moment that I saw it. How the house
stands sideways, for one thing; the front porch view
is of the lowland garden and the swamp,
not Mecox Road. I had them bring a crane
two years ago and excavate a pond.
There's no place you can stand and see the whole
of it, a trick that Brown used when he built
the lake at Stowe. The prospect from the knoll
where the house sits is very much like Stowe
sans folly and tempietto, though the plants
are all indigenous. Along the path
that winds down to the swamp, I've placed the reds:
bayberry in clumps, and trumpet-vines
on higher ground. I planted the tall reeds
myself, in hipboots, clearing out a years-
old jungle which is growing back so fast
I'll have to stock with Chinese grass carp, which
can grow to twenty pounds, a sort of Sumo
minnow that feeds on waterweeds. I hope
they don't eat lilypads. On the steep slope
beyond the pond's a sea of chicory;
it all goes blue next month. I've put some blue
lobelia there, too; off-blue, towards red.
The sequence of their blooming makes the view
change every week all summer. Light. Dark. Light.
It keeps the eye engaged with every step,
whether you want some inspiration or
a tussy-mussy (it's a word of Vita
Sackville-West's, means "wildflower bouquet."
I spent some hours making one today).

The path you can't see, over by the shed,
is verged by ailanthus; in a year
or three, the branches will have overgrown
to form a shady tunnel. At its end
I'll place another garden, which will block
the sight of houses going up like weeds
from here to Job's Lane Beach. At the high point
of their influence, Brown and Repton moved
whole villages whose jumble interfered
with one long view. *That's* capability.
Behind the ailanthus, in the woods,
I'll put in a spring garden by-and-by,
lady's slipper and jack-in-the-pulpit.
When you're heading down the hill or through
the meadow, there's no way you can tell, but
all the paths are spokes which lead you back
to one place, the lawn with the butternut
as hub, a spreading Tree of Life, as in
the *Roman de la Rose* or Genesis.
I wanted something right there for the eye
to focus on. Then I remembered Fairfield
Porter's painting called "July," with those
white Adirondack chairs. They're perfect there.
See how the white turns pale blue as the night
creeps in, full of mosquitoes and fireflies.
And don't be frightened by the strangled cries
from the swamp; those are peepers bellowing,
not *Psycho III*. The sounds and smells grow dense
this time of evening. The mock-tympanum
lugubriously beaten by the waves
a mile away sounds muffled in its quilt
of fog. The cooling air is redolent
of linden by the porch; its flowerets
will burst next week. I'll celebrate with friends,
throw a festival. The lurcher comes inside
and dampness clambers uphill from the pond
or blows in from the beachfront. There's a spot

of cloud against the night sky. Dark. Light. Dark.
It blossoms downward, filling up the yard.
Pretty soon your hand before your face
will be the farthest prospect you can see,
delight in. It's familiar by now,
the rote procession into night, and oddly
comforting, like music I recall:
a blues lament that all the things you loved
have disappeared, and you might as well be
anywhere, underlaid by gentle drums
that let you know you're near the ocean.

Healing the World From Battery Park

OM TARA
TU TARA
TURE SVAHA
   —TIBETAN MANTRA

Draw a deep breath. Hold it. Let it go.
That's the smell of the ocean.
Our forebears hailed from out there. There's a stele
to mark the spot where Minuit exchanged
a mess of beads and trinkets for this island.
He may have thought it proof he was
a clever trader, although if the sky
were sky-blue as today, the sunlight's flash
through bright glass would have been magnificent,
and that might have had tremendous value
in another culture. In another language,
"minuit"'s a division of the day.
I've divided my days among a host
of places near the sea. I get a lot
of comfort when I walk a beach, or through
the narrow streets among a crush of traders.
Sand in my shoes, sand of the Castle
Clinton courtyard where all of New York
turned out of yore to see the Jacksons,
Andrew and his wife. He'd whipped the bloody
British in the town of New Orleans
and massacred the Creeks. His steely eyes,
as blue as western skies, saw the space I see.
He breathed the same air. There's a little part
of him in me, that wants to drive away
the savages who populate the dark
expanse beyond the porch light's reach.
It takes a Trail of Tears to teach
that neighborhood improvement's not the point.
May the breath I draw become a balm
to soothe the exiled people of all times

---

and lands: the Cherokee, the Jew,
the people of Tibet whose loss brought us
abundant wisdom, the kulak and the Sioux,
the lover I abandoned and the friends
I drove away, the difficult and friendless
kicked out by their family, their school,
their church, their boss, their spouse, who found them too
impossible to put up with for one more minute.
In this park, their refuge, I divide my time
and feed it to the world when I exhale
like bread for ducks. It's not a fantasy
of power, and it's not about the rediscovery
of arcane treasure from a better place,
quieter and more romantic, like Tara
in the days of kings or in the antebellum
South. It's about the light that permeates
the sky above the boathouse where the sloop-
for-hire is moored. One romantic night,
it sailed across the harbor with my love
and me aboard. We drank champagne, and trailed
our fingers through the surface of the oil-
and-water stew that buoyed us. When we grew
apart, the two halves of a single wake
that break on banks across the dark expanse
of river from each other, I chose rage
to hold my sorrow's head beneath the waves
until I couldn't feel it anymore,
though somewhere under driftwood-littered slips
or in the trash-strewn slime a fathom down,
I knew that it was hiding. May the breath
I draw become a healing touch
to ease the pain I caused him, and to speed
the light that passed between and through us on
to its next stop. Here I divide my heart
among the teenaged couples and the shy
or clandestine romantics from the big
law firms who nuzzle on a bench, and queens

in stained Quiana shirts who cruise between
the slabs of stone with names of boys who died
in World War II. May it soothe my father,
who couldn't say how very much he loved
his wife, and all the tongue-tied men. And may
it heal the women, too; millions
like my mother who are left behind
when what they love about a man is wrenched
out of his body, hidden in another place.
In another language, "Tara" is the name
of a she-god sprung out of a human tear.
She heals all wounds and brings the world a sense
of peace. On this island where the gods
would outnumber the humans in a week if such
a mode of birth became habitual,
I beg her presence as I feel my breath
flying like a jet from Newark
out into the world. There's a quantity
of tenderness I feel sometimes
that drops into my chest precipitous
and golden as the sun into Fort Lee.
I couldn't tell you where it comes from, but
I'm learning where it hides. It's in the nectarine
you ate for breakfast, or the thing
you're doing now, not in what you think
you should do or in what comes next.
And it's not in what you think "God" means;
the only certainty is that you're wrong.
Draw a deep breath. Thank you, mother.
Hold the light inside and let it find
the ragged spots, a gentle tongue to probe
for caries. Then expire.
A little part of you is in the wind now,
a trace of pain or coffee in the scent
of brine that clasps you like a lover,
closer and more faithful than a lover.
Bless me, father. This is my first

---

confession: I'm living in the light
at the bottom of a sea of air,
everything I need in a place I share
with everyone. It's in your hands.

Acknowledgments

Acknowledgment is gratefully given to the following magazines, in which some of the poems in this book originally appeared:

American Letters and Commentary: "Harding's Beach"; *Brooklyn Review*: "Psalm" and "Spinner"; *Gandhabba*: "New Music"; *Hanging Loose*: "Healing the World From Battery Park," "Lit," "Summer, South Brooklyn," and "The Nineteenth Century Is 183 Years Old"; *Mag City*: "Desire Under the Pines," "From Journal" ("Picking up background material for a copy assignment . . ."), and "Solidarity"; *Santa Monica Review*: "The Morning"; *Shiny International*: "Film"; *Washington Review*: "Not Stravinsky" and "To Walter Lowenfels"; *The World*: "A Sense" and "Octavian."

"Four Organs," "Pretty Convincing," "The Fruit Streets," and "Words For Simone Weil" originally appeared in *BOMB*.

"July" and the last section of "King of the Wood" first appeared in *The Paris Review*.

"Close" and "Desire Under the Pines" appeared in the anthology *Son of the Male Muse*, published by The Crossing Press.

"This Much Fun" appeared in the catalog of *TV Generations*, an art exhibition at Los Angeles Contemporary Exhibitions.

"July" appeared in the catalog of *Earthly Delights: Garden Imagery in Contemporary Art*, an exhibition at Fort Wayne Museum of Art.

About the Author

Tim Dlugos grew up in East Longmeadow, Massachusetts and Arlington, Virginia, and attended LaSalle College in Philadelphia. He began publishing his poems in the early seventies, while living in Washington, D.C. In 1976, Dlugos relocated to New York City, where he quickly established himself as a prominent younger poet in the literary scene. His books include *G-9* (Hanuman Books), *Entre Nous* (Little Caesar Press), and *A Fast Life* (Sherwood Press). Throughout the eighties, Dlugos continued to publish his work in such magazines as *The Paris Review*, *BOMB*, and *Washington Review*. He was also a contributing editor of *Christopher Street* magazine. His work is included in *Poets For Life: Seventy-Six Poets Respond to AIDS* (Persea, 1992). Tim Dlugos died of AIDS on December 3, 1990, at the age of forty. At the time of his death, he was pursuing graduate studies at Yale Divinity School.

Also published by Amethyst Press

The Buried Body
Mark Ameen

"A unique and startling book . . . alternately fiercely cerebral, lean and wry, angry, funny, frighteningly self-conscious and tender." *OutWeek*

"Portrays one sexual man's sexual days with unrepentant rigor and detail." *The Advocate*

"To read through *The Buried Body*—cover to cover— is to put your head and emotions into the hands of an extraordinarily skillful poet, a writer you know you can trust." *Gay Community News*

"With a lesser poet we'd feel inundated, but despite the torrential downpour of words in about 200 pages of sheer energy, we feel refreshed by the force of a born wordslinger, a gifted storyteller, technically adept." *Lambda Book Report*

"I am amazed at this poet's gift and grateful for it. Reading him is like hearing a great voice in a singer. It's as if I could see it, touch it: a voice naked on a stage in a hot, exposing light." JOAN LARKIN

Poetry
$10.95 paper
ISBN 0-927200-04-X

Also published by Amethyst Press

Discontents: New Queer Writers
Edited by Dennis Cooper

Discontents is an anthology of new short fiction by a loosely knit group of lesbian and gay writers whose work transgresses, rejects and sometimes parodies the concerns of mainstream gay-identified fiction. In certain cases this takes the form of a post-moral examination of fetishistic sexual practices; in others post-modern techniques are brought into play as a way of reframing and subverting traditional notions of romantic/sexual loves; in still others intense emotion is allowed to overwhelm narrative, resulting in stories that ring far truer to individual life experience than the prevalent homogenized norm which puts "coming out" and "gay identification" at the center of "our existence." Sexy, political, non-separatist, experimental, crude, literary, wild, often all at the same time, these writers' works represent a fresh, daring yet very reader-friendly sensibility that extends the notion of gay literature toward the unforeseeable future.

"Here, in a maelstrom of more than 50 transgressive works—from charming cartoon to vicious lampoon, from experimental fiction to extraordinarily personal AIDS stories—we can see and feel, perhaps for the first time in 20 years, the sheer unlimited potential of queer writing."   *The Advocate*

Fiction
$12.95 paper
ISBN 0-927200-10-4

Also published by Amethyst Press

Idols
Dennis Cooper

"Dennis Cooper has united Eros and Apollo—the boy who is love and the man who is poetry—and in the process written some of the sexiest, loveliest verse I've ever read."   EDMUND WHITE

"*Idols* is a seasoned book—the poems are varied and skillfully crafted, and the motif of adolescent sexual yearning is not all that unconnected with the fantasies of adolescents grown old. Cooper is frank about his sexuality, his hustles, his loves. His idols include the famous and the not-so-famous: a series of teen-age gods with first names only appear, as do various turn-ons who are well-known: Peter Frampton, John F. Kennedy, Jr., the Cassidy brothers. Cooper hits us where we live; he is a young poet of startling gifts."
San Francisco Review of Books

Poetry
$8.95 paper
ISBN 0-927200-00-7

Also published by Amethyst Press

Horse and Other Stories
Bo Huston

"Bo Huston's first book . . . is a damn impressive read—it's filled with good stories, fascinating characters, some moral imperatives, and everywhere, the mysteries of human behavior."   *Manifest Reader*

"*Horse and Other Stories* is a coup for Bo Huston, who has a disturbing, seductive, and ultimately addictive voice. Marginals are his obsession—drug addicts, hustlers, irritable faggots, oblivious debutantes, and bemused recluses—he makes them sympathetic, believable, almost heroic."   *The Village Voice*

"In *Horse*, Huston has captured the worlds of the disaffected, the disinherited, and the disinterested. In language that is often as stark as the individuals and places he describes, Huston shows again the importance of literature in defining our realities."

The Advocate

"*Horse and Other Stories* is the quintessential gay book of the 90s—a book which need not be gay to be good but certainly is a reflection of the best writing coming out of the gay community today."   *OutWeek*

"A string of pearls."   Sarah Schulman

Fiction
$9.95 paper
ISBN 0-927200-03-1

Also published by Amethyst Press

Remember Me
Bo Huston

"A fascinating and touching study of an intimate, obsessive relationship. For all its subdued and sad elements, *Remember Me* is a thoroughly hopeful and compelling story about the mysterious boundaries of friendship and love. This is one you'll want to read again—buy it, read it and keep it." DOROTHY ALLISON

" . . . a gentle and serene book about AIDS, as well as an in-depth treatment of an unconventional friendship . . . Most striking about this short novel is the way it subtly integrates the narrator's HIV infection into the everyday fabric of life. And the central relationship in the book, between a gay male and a female recluse, defies all categories." *OutWeek*

"A stark and reflective novel, it tries desperately to offer small moments of hope in an otherwise cruel and vicious world." *Lambda Book Report*

"*Remember Me* is a leap, not only for its depiction of AIDS but also for Huston's development as an artist. As in much fiction by people with AIDS, the reader can sense Huston's desire to stretch, to race against the clock in an effort to reach insight through simplicity. 'Will I be alive long enough to mature?' the protagonist asks. Judging from this novel, the answer is yes." *The Village Voice*

Fiction
$9.95 paper
ISBN 0-927200-08-2

Also published by Amethyst Press

Bedrooms Have Windows
Kevin Killian

"With a dazzling prose line that recalls his debut work, *Shy*, Kevin Killian's *Bedrooms Have Windows* will, I predict, continue its author's meteoric rise to fame as one of the newest and brightest stars in the sex/experimental writing firmament that includes Acker, Cooper, Glück, and Gooch. *Bedrooms Have Windows* combines glittering suburban surfaces with dark sexual secrets in a storyline that's as moral as it is novel. In the end, it's the secrets of the human heart, rather than depictions of sexual desperadoes, that will mean most to us. If you care about sex, or writing—or both!—read this book."   BRUCE BOONE

Fiction
$9.95 paper
ISBN 0-927200-01-5

Also published by Amethyst Press

Three Views From Vertical Cliffs
Eric Latzky

"Elegant and highly constructed . . . I like the ways in which Latzky is attempting to expand the novelistic form in order to bring to life characters whom I can recognize." KATHY ACKER

". . . dark, broad strokes . . . a static balance between the chaos of life and the limits of a canvas, between boundless passion and the comforts of intimacy . . ." *Publishers Weekly*

"With an unprecedented immediacy and revelation. . . the novel is consistently engaging. *Three Views From Vertical Cliffs* is reminiscent of Edgar Allan Poe's ruminative gothic tales with their unnamed but palpable psychological horrors." *The Advocate*

Fiction
$9.95 paper
ISBN 0-927200-11-2

Also published by Amethyst Press

This Every Night
Patrick Moore

"Blithely descending into an intriguing, shadowy underworld, *This Every Night* may well fan already-raging political flames. It's no pedantic tale of doing the right thing. Patrick Moore writes a brave, low literature of the bottom." *Interview Magazine*

"Read *This Every Night* for its beautiful prose, for its walk on the gritty side of sex, for its convincing hatred that generates wild humor and disgust. Moore describes a tumultuous gay world—this world can sell you a one-way ticket to the void, but it also can provide the opposite, the balm and sweetness of community." ROBERT GLÜCK

"Once I started reading I couldn't stop and I wished the story would never come to an end."
KAREN FINLEY

Fiction
$9.95 paper
ISBN 0-927200-06-6

Also published by Amethyst Press

Hand Over Heart: Poems 1981-1988
David Trinidad

"David Trinidad's desolate homages to American culture are perfect bullets fired from two inches away."   MARY GAITSKILL

"Superfan Trinidad's slyly personal writing puts us onstage with girl groups, in front of TV rerun haikus, and in the bedroom dancing alone to singles spinning in free verse. But underlying the fascination with electric glitter is the innocence and uncertainty of a life marked with addictions and the guarded search for gay love at a time when love has been defined by *The Munsters* and the Supremes."   *City Pages*

"Trinidad's poems read like declarations of independence, epistles of personal choice . . . He turns old 45s on a new edge."   *Voice Literary Supplement*

"*Hand Over Heart* is a brave and beautiful book. Trinidad has exposed himself, his experience, and his feelings in a manner rare in modern poetry."
The James White Review

Poetry
$9.95 paper
ISBN 0-927200-07-4